Since 1840 each President of the United States who has been elected during a year ending in zero has not left office alive.

WILLIAM HENRY HARRISON
Elected in 1840. *Died while in office—1841—* of pneumonia and pleurisy.

ABRAHAM LINCOLN
Elected in 1860. Reelected in 1864. *Died while in office—1865—by an assassin's bullet.*

JAMES ABRAM GARFIELD
Elected in 1880. *Died while in office—1881—* by an assassin's bullet.

WILLIAM McKINLEY
Elected in 1900. *Died while in office—1901—* by an assassin's bullet.

WARREN GAMALIEL HARDING
Elected in 1920. *Died while in office—1923—* of pneumonia and heart trouble.

FRANKLIN DELANO ROOSEVELT
Elected in 1940 (his third term). *Died while in office—1945—of a cerebral hemorrhage.*

JOHN FITZGERALD KENNEDY
Elected in 1960. *Died while in office—1963—* by an assassin's bullet(s).

- **Has this death cycle been an incredible coincidence of historic proportions?**
- **Why has each of these cases been shrouded in mystery?**
- **Is there—as some historians have concluded—a plot or plan involved?**

D1399939

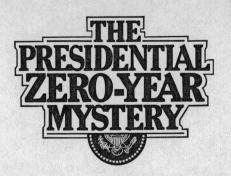